YÁAMAY

An Anthology of Feminine Perspectives Across Indigenous California

YÁAMAY

An Anthology of Feminine Perspectives Across Indigenous California

Edited by
Camaray Davalos
Avelaka Macarro
Rebecca Macarro

GREAT OAK PRESS
PECHANGA, CALIFORNIA

ISBN: 978-1-942279-34-1 (pbk.)
ISBN: 978-1-942279-35-8 (E-Book)

Front Cover Image: Kúutpat. Courtesy of Alexis Munoa Dyer.

Library of Congress Control Number: 2023940110

Printed in the United States of America.

Great Oak Press
P.O. Box 1477
Temecula, CA, 92593
www.greatoakpress.com

Royalties from the sale of this book will be used to support Strong Hearted Native Women's Coalition, Inc. and their vision to empower people with the tools for independence, courage, and a strong direction to make healthy life choices for themselves, their children, and family.

Strong Hearted Native Women's Coalition, Inc.
P.O. Box 2488 - Valley Center, CA 92082-2488
Office: 760-644-4781 - Fax: 760-477-5993
Website: www.strongheartednativewomen.org
Like us on: www.facebook.com/SHNWCInc
Donations: http://www.gofundme.com/stronghearted

"I am like nothing they've seen, and cannot be contained. I am untouchable here, not because I am fragile, because I am fierce."

—April Bouchard, from her poem titled, '1995'.

REX
PURE LARD

This book is dedicated to our human and non-human relatives of past, present, and future, whose stories coat the inside of our minds and souls; who have fought and endured, and will continue to do so.

Leona Qéengish
Pechanga Tribe, 1909.
San Diego History Center.
Great-great-great-grandmother of Camaray, Avelaka, and Rebecca, whose legacy endures with us.

Table of Contents

Wólnish

$ó'a

Preface

By Avelaka Macarro

Native women have never been alone in our experiences. This collective of poems, essays, and short stories only prove the universality of our struggles. With this collection of pieces, *Yáamay*, which means 'to endure' in Chamtéela, shows the universality of our struggles. We carry our past with us, with the joy of our ancestry compounded with the trauma of genocide and colonialism. Much of our inspiration for creating this book came from personal stories and documents of the Native existence, like the excerpts from *Yumáyk Yumáyk*, written by Villiana Hyde. The continuation of Indigenous cultures has relied on the strengths of our women, despite every attempt to injure, assault, and silence us. It is with this understanding that we separated the pieces into the four natural parts of our story: Tówla, Kúp, Wólnish, and $ó'a.

The first half of this anthology focuses on how women carry their history in all things. We open the anthology with the story of the frog woman, "Siny Hantak: Frog Woman" by Theresa Gregor, to remind us of the struggle and sacrifice of our ancestors. The Frog Woman, an Indigenous Circe, propelled our existence and civilization with her revenge on Wuyóot. The first chapter Tówla, meaning root, acts as a memory of our ties to the earth we have lived on since time immemorial; the ancestral origin to the peoples, tribes, waters, and lands. Like "Siny Hantak: Frog Woman", these poems respect the physical and mythological origins of our people across Southern California. They are not all positive reflections, but they do reflect the raw experience of our Native heritage.

The period of dormancy, or Kúp, reflects the moments of loss and thievery on the part of colonial governance; the time where we were nearly erased from existence. This affected every Indigenous person in the Americas, and much of our culture was systematically destroyed. We became "survivors", as described in Megan Dorame's "Sweet Oranges". Her depiction of the Spanish missionaries describes all of the institutional decomposition of Native people, particularly in the United

States, where forced assimilation continues to affect modern Indigenous folx. To quote Meadow Fuller's "Best Picture", "we're tired" because we move forward with the worry of not knowing our full culture or history. For a long time, we existed as an unknown and dormant minority, but no longer.

Moving into the 21st century has left a lot of transition for the Native communities in North America. The Wólnish chapter (meaning "cultivate") is the center of our current reality, and how we continue to grow through our varied interpretations of Indigenous life. A large part of this experience is on reservations or as Urban Natives, as depicted in "1995" by April Bouchard and "The Rez" by Nichole Vasquez-Sutter. We are not struggling with the loss described in Kúp, but rather redesigning what Native culture and life looks like under the American regime. Fitting our names, hair, language, homes, and bodies into this world comes with an added resilience. We are cultivating ourselves with so many layers of past and adjusting to the mold of modernity as Indigenous women and femmes.

The "bloom" of our lives finalizes in $ó'a, as we identify and burrow in the strength of our narratives and self-worth. The connection to nature is a key part of this chapter, as we consider ourselves stewards of the land and water surrounding all tribal territory. Marlene' Dusek writes that "this relationship is an old one, A natural one" in "Regeneration", describing the ties of the Indigenous people and this land. As it grows, we grow. Recognizing this connection is key to our narrative and how we assert sovereignty and reassert our belonging in these spaces. Our link to the Earth and our past stories is essential as our future flourishes.

The translations included below these chapter titles come from the first text I had contact with that translated Chamtéela[1] to English. *Yumáyk Yumáyk* told the oral history of Villiana Hyde, a member of the Rincon Band of Luiseño Indians. As a

[1] 'Chamtéela' translates to 'Our language'. This is the word Payómkawish people use to refer to our Native language, as we move away from settler-colonial terminology.

child, Villiana was forced to attend Sherman Indian Boarding School, whose philosophy of assimilation mirrored that of R. H. Pratt's, "Kill the Indian in him, and save the man". Villiana worked to protect and enrich her community by recording her language, and we pay our respects to her work by including the passages in this book.

The devastation of our tribes, our lost people, our fragmented languages, our missing women, and our untold stories came together in the journey of this anthology. Until recently, Indigenous women and femme-identifying persons had often been left out of the warrior narrative. In reading and editing these works, it is clear to see that we have been (and continue to be) the backbone of Native resilience. We endure with respect and love for our ancestors whose perseverance made this anthology possible.

To continue the fight for recognition, sovereignty, and respect, it is the editors' intention that the majority of proceeds are donated to organizations dedicated to empowering and healing the Indigenous nations affected by gender and sexual violence. It is also our intention that this work mobilizes the sovereign rights to our physical bodies, lands, and waters that have previously been exploited by colonial violence.

As we journey forward with the literary and artistic expressions of our Southern California Indigenous women and feminine-identifying people, we defy the expectations of the modern world. We will raise our children in the language of the Earth. We will bathe in the water of the ancient floods. We will write with the blood of our ancestors and the hopes of the next seven generations. We will march for our rights. We will mourn for our losses and the traditions we do not know. We will not be cornered away from the history of genocide. We will stand and remember the purpose of our birth. We will be here. We are here. And so shall we stay.

Acknowledgments

We would like to acknowledge Great Oak Press Director, Editor-in-Chief, Lauren Niezgodzki, for being our compass, from coordinating our meetings, to helping us delegate tasks, to returning to this project with encouragement after the pandemic.

We also could not do this without Alexis Munoa Dyer and Andrew Dyer for their creative design expertise that remained faithful to our vision, and to Alexis specifically for her contributions to the cover and bio photos. Thank you to Myra Masiel-Zamora for her role as our liaison, her attention to detail, and her work in finding culturally relevant imagery that enhanced this book greatly; Nichole Vasquez-Sutter's thoughtful contribution to the creation of this book's subtitle.

Thank you to all of our tribal community who were involved in the creation of the Great Oak Press, allowing us to put forth works that represent ourselves; and to Villiana Hyde, for her literary endeavors and astute frankness which inspired us greatly.

To all the contributors of this anthology, we are eternally grateful for your patience, commitment, and belief in this project. To our ancestors who loved us before they knew us; to our loved ones who are no longer with us; and to our friends and family who have always been in our corner, cham$úun lóoviwun 'óomik.

Editor's Note

The chapter titles and quotes in this anthology are from fellow Payómkawish writer and language keeper, Villiana Hyde, from her book *Yumáyk Yumáyk*. Our language has been called "Luiseño", a word made by Spanish missionaries. In an effort to return to our native language, we prefer the name Chamtéela ("Our language") or 'Áataxum pomtéela ("The peoples' language"). You will find words in various pieces that use Chamtéela, but many others use the native language of their respective peoples' from the region.

Introduction

By Camaray Davalos

Indigenous people have lived in what is now known as Southern California since time immemorial. Long before European settlers put monetary value on land, before miners destructively pressurized hillsides with water in search of gold, and before domesticated animals grazed native vegetation to near extinction, Indigenous peoples of Southern California had developed their own complex governments, social structures, and land management practices. Before the Spanish established the mission system and coerced Indigenous peoples into becoming Catholic neophytes, complex religions had already been practiced. Elaborate trading systems had been established. Intricate star systems had been studied and named.

What can be described as tribes of Southern California changes depending on which anthropologist is delineating our borders. When remembering that California is a state created through settler colonialism via the United States, we better understand that lines of 'north', 'central' and 'south' can be arbitrary.[1] But there are roughly nine distinct peoples of what is known as Southern California, each with varied bands and villages extending from them.[2] From the northernmost region are the Chumash, meaning 'bead maker', whose territory spans from San Luis Obispo to Los Angeles counties on the coast, and inland to the edge of the San Joaquin Valley. Going south are the Kitanemuk, meaning 'Those of the nest (house)', whose territory is located in what is now known as Kern County, in the foothills of the Sierra Nevada mountains. Southward are the Tataviam, 'People Facing the Sun', whose territories span the so-called Ventura and Los Angeles Counties. Directly east are the Yuhaaviatam,[3] or 'People of the Pines', whose territory

---

[1] The way in which these territories have been listed are modern territories and not necessarily our complete ancestral territories.

[2] It is important to note that many of these territories extend further than what is described here, frequently overlapping into others.

[3] Also known as the Serrano, a Spanish term meaning 'highlander'.

is currently known as San Bernardino County. Southwest are the Tongva,[4] 'People of the Earth', where so-called Los Angeles County takes space.

Directly south of the Tongva are the Acjachemen,[5] 'People who pile on top of one another', in the coastal region of so-called Orange County. South of the Acjachemen are the Payómkawichum,[6] 'People of the West', whose traditional territory spans western Riverside County and north San Diego County. East of the Payómkawichum are the Kuupangaxwichem, 'People who slept here', whose traditional space is also in so-called San Diego County. Farther east are the Ivilyuqaletem,[7] whose large territory spans much of Riverside County towards the Mojave. South of the Ivilyuqaletem are the Kumeyaay, 'The people who stand over the cliffs', with a territory spanning broadly throughout San Diego, starting at the shores of the Pacific Ocean, going north to the waterways shared with Payómkawichum and Kuupangaxwichem, south into Baja California Mexico, and east inland to where the Colorado River once ran and whose waterways are shared by the Kumeyaay, KwaTsaan and Cocopah. To the far east are the Kwatsáan,[8] 'Those who descended', whose original territory spans not just Southern California, but Arizona and Baja Mexico.[9] Spanning across borders of California and Arizona are the Halchidhoma, 'People who live toward the water' and

[4] Also known as Gabrieleno. Names with the ending 'eno' were conceived by Spanish Missionaries to denote these groups, and more recently many of these groups have shed said terms to instead use their tribe's own language to refer to themselves. Henceforth, these "mission tribes" will be referred to by the ancestral names they called themselves, as an act of decolonizing identity.

[5] Also known as Juaneno.

[6] Also known as Luiseno.

[7] Also known as Cahuilla, another term that was reconstructed by the Spanish.

[8] Also known as Quechan.

[9] In efforts to be inclusive to those who submitted, we accepted a joint submission from Tule River Yokut descendants, who are on the verge of southern and central California. Due to differing views of where "Southern California" ends, we feel it's appropriate to include Tule River Yokut descendants in this book.

Pipa Aha Macav,[10] 'People by the river'.

What makes these tribes regionally distinct to Southern California is their relationship with the flora and terrain sharing space with them. The intricately woven coil baskets made of *Juncus textilis* only flourish in this specific region, and are synonymous with Southern California Indian art. The unmistakably dome shaped homes made of willow or tule, brush of the drought deciduous shrublands, spanned Chumash lands all the way down to Kumeyaay territory. Dependence on chaparral and desert plants chia (*Salvia columariae*), yucca, and pine nuts (*Pinus quadrifolia*) are also unique to the region. And of course, no California Indigenous diet would be complete without acorns, no matter the region.

Indigenous peoples of the area formed ways to enhance the fertility of landscapes, using scientific knowledge on par with cultures from around the world. The Kumeyaay, Kuupangaxwichem,[11] and Payómkawichum, as well as other tribes of the region, would use burning techniques to enhance edible plant productivity and to bring out new shoots used for basket weaving. By keeping track of seasonal changes of the sun, for instance, the Iviluqaletem and Chumash peoples were able to ascertain the availability of certain plants and animals for their needs. Some Ivilyuqaletem were able to gauge the sun's light, moving a stick as a dial to study times at which certain seeds were ripe, birds made nests, and when plants sprouted.[12] It is important to note that many of these people, indeed, still use these techniques today and hold ceremonies that honor the changing seasons.

Indigenous peoples of this region had perfected fine art, and continue to do so in contemporary times. Basketry, pottery, and other utilitarian works made of stone and shell are still created by Indigenous descendants and highly prized by

[10] Also known as the Mojave tribe.
[11] Also known as *Dieguenо* and *Cupeno*, respectively.
[12] Anderson, M. Kat. "Tending the Wild: Native American Knowledge and the Management of California's Natural Resources". 1st ed., University of California Press, 2005.

collectors today. This adept knowledge of how to live among the landscape, grow food, and procure medicine from flora and fauna is how Indigenous peoples of Southern California were able to maintain a population more dense than any space of equal size in North America at the time of European arrival.[13]

Just as Southern California tribes share segments of rich culture, we have also shared a traumatic past. The first mission, Mission San Diego de Alcalá, was built by Spanish missionaries in 1769 on Kumeyaay land,[14] against the will of the Kumeyaay. Twenty-one Franciscan missions, along with Spanish military posts, were constructed throughout California, built with the involuntary labor of Indigenous inhabitants. Indigenous people were coerced or outright forced into Catholic conversion within the missions, and padres drove them into labor to maintain the missions and associated crops, with no pay and filthy, bacteria-breeding conditions. Physical abuse at the hands of missionaries and Spanish soldiers was common, as was mental and spiritual abuse through indoctrination by the church. A 1775 letter from friar Junipero Serra to his military commander underscores the oppressiveness of Franciscan missionaries:

> *I am sending them to you so that a period of exile, and two or three whippings which Your Lordship may order applied to them on different days, may serve, for them and for the rest, for a warning, may be of spiritual benefit to all; and this last is the prime motive of our work. If Your Lordship does not have shackles, with your permission they may be sent from here.*[15]

---

[13] Gutiérrez, Ramón A. "Contested Eden: California Before the Gold Rush, Published in Association with the California Historical Society". Edited by RAMÓN A. GUTIÉRREZ et al., 1st ed., University of California Press, 1998.

[14] Present day Old Town San Diego.

[15] Castillo, Elias author. A Cross of Thorns: The Enslavement of California's Indians by the Spanish Missions. Fresno, California: Craven Street Books, 2015.

Of course, many of our Indigenous ancestors fought back against these oppressive mission systems. One of the most direct instances was the revolt at Mission San Diego de Alcalá by the Kumeyaay. In the early morning hours of November 5, 1775, warriors from about fifteen surrounding villages attacked the poorly guarded mission, ultimately killing Father Jayme. Afterwards, they set the mission ablaze. This attack "weakened Spain's already tenuous hold on its northern territory",[16] and showed how far Indigenous people would go to defend their own, and to defy foreign powers.

Still, much of the life our ancestors knew changed dramatically. New diseases strained the health of Indigenous peoples, causing the death of thousands in only a few decades. Catholicism sought to uproot traditional religions of the various bands, and as a result many important songs and ceremonial protocol were lost or used in secret. By the mid-1830s, the Mexican government secularized the missions, thus breaking apart the lands they were built upon to be sold or given to private citizens. Although it was the end of the mission era, Indigenous lands were immediately seized by Mexico and Indigenous peoples often lived out their lives in servitude. After the Mexican-American War, the terms of the Treaty of Guadalupe Hidalgo (1848) were put into effect and California became a U.S. territory.

1848 was also the year gold was discovered near Sutter's Mill in Northern California. Very little mining took place in Southern California during this time, but Indigenous populations in this region were entangled nonetheless. The demand for food to be grown and sent up to Northern California's mining population increased, and ranches and farms in Southern California grew exponentially, pushing tribes farther towards the boundaries of their homelands. It was common for Indigenous peoples of this region to be evicted from their homes in order to make room for non-Native ranchers. Indigenous people

[16] Carrico, Richard L. "Sociopolitical Aspects of the 1775 Revolt at Mission San Diego De Alcala." *The Journal of San Diego History*, vol. 43, no. 3, 1997, https://doi.org/https://sandiegohistory.org/journal/1997/july/missionrevolt/.

had chosen to situate villages where their own crops could be fruitful, or where the best gathering sites were, and this was often near water. Land speculators knew this and illegally removed Indigenous people from these fertile areas, replacing villages with ranchos. In one harrowing example of this, the Tongva were promised approximately 1.2 million acres, including the 50,000 acreage that was the San Sebastian Reserve. The 50,000 acres of the San Sebastian Reserve was never taken into trust for the tribe, and instead became integrated into Tejon Ranch, owned by Superintendent of Indian Affairs Edward Beale.[17]

Once California became a state in 1850, our ancestors were subjected not only to the chaos of settlers' whims, but to the state government's dehumanizing policies. Notable was California's, "An Act for the Government and Protection of Indians", which, despite its seemingly benevolent name, legalized the servitude of Indigenous people and allowed settlers "to have the care, custody, control and earnings of such [Indian] minor until he or she obtain the age of majority." Later on, this act was amended to allow Indigenous adults to be indentured in the same way. White settlers used these acts to enslave Indigenous people, and when the California Legislature authorized monies for the suppression of Indian hostilities, "these payments only encouraged Whites to form volunteer companies and try to eliminate all the Indians in California."[18] In other words, the state government's sanctioning of genocide of Indigenous people was born in conjunction with the violence of white vigilantes, with state legislators passing "three bills in the 1850s that raised up to $1.51 million to fund these operations — a great deal of money at the time — for past and future anti-Indian militia operations."[19] From 1850 to 1861, governors called for at least 24 state militia expeditions, which claimed the lives of at least 1,340 California Indians, while it is estimated vigilantes killed

[17] http://www.gabrielinotribe.org/historical-sites-1/

[18] Dutschke, Dwight. "A History of American Indians in California: Introduction". *Five Views: An Ethnic Historic Site Survey for California.* October 8, 2014.

[19] Madley, Benjamin. "It's time to acknowledge the genocide of California's Indians." *Los Angeles Times.* May 22, 2016.

roughly 6,460 of our ancestors.[20]

The nefarious boarding school era spearheaded by the Federal government, began in the mid to late 1800s. This assimilation agenda grew out of the United State's need to quell "Indian hostilities", which were brought forth and escalated by settler violence and land theft. The rationale to bring Native people into white civilization through education was outlined by the Indian Peace Commission on January 7, 1868:

> *Through sameness of language is produced the sameness of sentiment and thought; customs and habits are moulded and assimilated in the same way, and thus in process of time the differences producing trouble would have been gradually obliterated.*

Of course, part of this rationale depended on settler's viewpoint of Indigenous people as inherently barbaric; if only Indigenous people were educated in civilized ways, ways of the white settlers, then the problems of resistance and defiance would disappear. Thus when boarding schools were formed, Indigenous children were often forcibly removed from their homes, taken to dormitories far away, and expected to speak English and learn domestic chores in the white man's way. Many were abused physically, emotionally, or sexually, and some of these traumas have passed onto present-day descendants.

It must be stressed that Indigenous people of Southern California did not willingly accept these years of mistreatment. There were countless instances of rebellion, and actions taken to undo the traumas of colonization. An important example was one of the first major grassroots political organizations, The Mission Indian Federation. In 1919 the Mission Indian Federation (MIF) was created, comprising members of groups including the Payómkawichum, Kuupangaxwichem, Kumeyaay, Ivilyuqaletem, Yuhaaviatam, Tongva, and Acjachemen. The main focus of the MIF was for Native people to gain citizenship in the United States in order

[20] Ibid.

to shed their ward status and become truly sovereign over their lands. Attaining equality with white settlers, and abolishing the Bureau of Indian Affairs (BIA), who sought to control Native ownership of land and freedoms, were equally important. In 1924, citizenship was finally granted to all Indigenous people. The work that the MIF and other Indigenous rights groups performed was no doubt significant as far as attaining elements of sovereignty and reducing BIA authority on reservations, and the MIF remained an organization into the early 1970s.

In 1953 Indian Termination Policies were implemented throughout the United States, revoking federal recognition for numerous tribes while stripping rights away from those who remained recognized or who were never recognized to begin with. For the tribes whose recognition was revoked, land ownership was divided and sold, with proceeds going to the tribe; federal programs for tribes were stopped; and tribal sovereignty was diminished since "the loss of the land base meant that in most cases the tribe had no geographic area to exert jurisdiction."[21] Furthermore, Public Law 280 (1953) extended criminal and civil jurisdiction to the state of California, shifting the power over recognized and non-recognized tribes from the federal government to the states. To be sure, PL-280 did not take criminal or civil jurisdiction away from tribal governments; tribes can still establish their own courts, and create and enforce tribal laws on their reservations.[22]

Many tribes have persisted, if not flourished, since. Landmark court cases, like *Cabazon v. California* affirm that tribes in California have the ability to regulate gambling on reservation land. Since then, tribes have diversified their forms of revenue and through these enterprises have been able to reclaim ancestral lands in efforts to halt outside development, protect sacred sites into perpetuity, form language immersion schools, and administer family and social services. In other acts of defiance against settler-colonial powers, tribes like

[21] Getches,D., & Wilkinson, C. (2011). *Cases and Materials on Federal Indian Law*, 6th ed., St. Paul, MN: West Publishing Co.
[22] Ibid.

the Tongva have taken educational sovereignty into their own hands and engaged institutions like the University of California, Los Angeles to form accurate curriculum and information on the Tongva and Indigenous history of the state in general. The passing of California Assembly Bill 738 is another testament to the hard work of California Indigenous educators, as it requires the state to adopt and apply curriculum based on Native American, specifically California Native, studies.

Today, one of the most pressing issues for Indigenous peoples of Southern California is protecting land from the ever constant threat of development. Indigenous people of the region have developed ingenious ways to protect and manage their lands, despite colonial efforts to subvert them. Through the implementation of land conservancies like the Native American Land Conservancy, which is based out of Indio, CA, Indigenous people have been able to protect and restore sacred sites of the Inland Empire, Coachella Valley, and Morongo Basin. In 2012, the Pechanga Tribe saved their sacred Pu'éska mountain from desecration at the hands of a granite quarry by purchasing the mountain and later putting it into trust by the federal government. Even individual tribal members have attained land, creating spaces where Indigenous relatives can meet to learn, gather Native plants, and engage in other traditional practices on their ancestral territory. Tribes have also maintained their position as stewards of not only the land but of the waters, securing their sovereign claim to water rights by any means necessary. The Agua Caliente Band of Cahuilla Indians, for instance, set a momentous precedent when it was established that their reserved water rights also applied to groundwater.[23]

»»»

Much of the content in this anthology highlights the histories specific to the Indigenous people of Southern California, and Indigenous peoples' shared experiences as a whole. The

[23] Agua Caliente Band of Cahuilla Indians v. Coachella Valley Water District, 849 F.3d 1262 (9th Cir. 2017)

California Mission system that extended its influence over our ancestors has been inspiration for some of the poetry in this text; lateral oppression, which, among various reasons, has stemmed from loss of culture due to assimilationist policies and settler violence, is another matter that has inspired pieces in this book. The multifarious effects of colonization have reverberated throughout the communities of Southern California Indigenous people, and can still be felt today. Many of us are figuring out how to cope with these less than ideal circumstances. However many of the pieces in this anthology focus not only on colonial implications, but on ancestral stories, growing up on the rez, and the joys of (self) love and independence. Using self-expression through art has helped us to understand our lives, or at the very least, articulate our experiences as Indigenous people.

Over the years, there have been tiny flames in corners of Southern California Indian country, places where voices of our people have been magnified through text and art. We pay homage to those women, femmes, and nonbinary and gender fluid relatives who have paved the way for us, allowing themselves to be both vulnerable and brave in sharing their lives with the world. There have been some books, written by elders long since passed, which have greatly influenced us. *Yumáyk Yumáyk* by Villiana Hyde (Payómkawish and Kumeyaay) is a stunning collection of autobiographical and ethnographic literature; *Delfina Cuero: Her Autobiography-An Account of Her Last Years and Her Ethnobotanic Contributions* by Delfina Cuero (Kumeyaay) is at once a harrowing account of California Indigenous life in the early 1900s, and a guide on native plant knowledge and uses; *Not for Innocent Ears: Spiritual Traditions of a Desert Cahuilla Medicine Woman* by Ruby Modesto (Desert Cahuilla), an incredibly intimate autobiography of a woman who came into her healing powers at age 40.

More recently, authors such as Deborah A. Miranda (Chumash and Esselen) and Myra Masiel-Zamora (Payómkawish) have contributed to contemporary literature and academia, analyzing pre-contact life and rewriting settler-colonial narratives with their own personal narratives. Desiree Wetz (Acjachemen/Payómkawish), Jo. A. Garcia (Payómkawish) and Nichole Vasquez-Sutter (Payómkawish) have contributed to the realm of children's literature, creating books where Native youth see their stories and culture reflected. Jessa Calderon (Tongva/Chumash) has tapped into young adult literature with *SisterHood*, a novel which courageously tackles modern issues Native girls face. Cindi Alvitre (Tongva), Barbara Drake (Tongva), Tima Lotah Link (Chumash), Heidi Lucero (Acjachemen/Mutsun Ohlone), and Lorene Sisquoc (Cahuilla/Fort Sill Apache), all part of the Chia Cafe Collective, have published recipe books on native California foods and the philosophy behind cultural survival and sustainability. Poets like Kelly Caballero (Tongva), Emily Clarke (Cahuilla) and Megan Dorame (Tongva) have engaged audiences with prose readings, shows, and workshops, establishing a solid Indigenous presence in major Southern California cities. Artists such as Weshoyot Alvitre (Tongva), L. Frank Manriquez (Tongva/Ajacheman), and Alexis Munoa Dyer (Payómkawish) have bestowed the world with visual art that embodies a defiance against the colonial narrative, much of which comes in the form of graphic novel illustrations, photography, and other mixed media. Many of Yáamay's contributors are not self-described poets or artists, but they embody this persona nonetheless.

As a recent graduate majoring in Native American Studies, I was positively overwhelmed by the amount of Indigenous women authors who were taught in my courses. Some writers wrote fiercely about their roles as leaders in their communities, who were compelled to protect sacred lands from natural resource exploitation. Others wrote of their conflicting experiences as someone of mixed-ancestry, simply trying to find their place in the modern world. As I went through classes reading various works, I could not help but notice the lack of Southern California voices. I believe there are universal experiences shared by all Indigenous peoples that we gravitate towards. Reading about and sharing these experiences encourage us to better understand the plights we face, and help us feel less alone. But there are also voices and realities that are distinct to each community, and it is only those people who can speak of them from a place of raw pain and beauty. That is how it is for our Payómkawish people.

Of course, I understood this lack of representation was not a slight from my professors, but rather a reflection of the lack of resources, representation, and outlets some of our people have. I have talked to some Southern California Indigenous people who consider themselves highly private; they simply do not feel comfortable sharing their stories. On the other hand, many Indigenous writers who are published have completed higher levels of education, and thus feel more confident with their writing. Even so, academic success is not synonymous with writing ability, talent in penning poetry or creating stunning visual art. It is evident that we need creative expression from all segments of Indigenous Southern California society because it gives a more nuanced representation of our realities, dreams, and musings. If you have a longing to tell a story or speak from the soul, nothing can stop it from pouring out. This anthology comes from the utmost urgency to tell our stories through writing and visual art, whether it be poetry, photography, or something in-between. As we move further into contemporary times, published pieces from our Southern California Indigenous people are infrequent if not non-existent. Now is the time for us to tell our stories before they are written for us by anthropologists, archeologists, historians, or non-Indians.

When we write for ourselves and tell our own stories, we remind the world that we are still present, existing, and resisting. We are not a part of history, but rather a continuously flourishing community of modern Indigenous people who march defiantly into the future.

Tówla *(Root)*

Má'matum hísh pom'onániy 'atáxmi Indiomi cháami wuníyk pi' michá''axáninik chamqálqatumi michá''axáninik chóo'on híicha pomíiqala yumáyk. Pí'sum híingay qáy yumáyk tuvyúngax?"

"They are going to want to know about how we Indians lived, about how everything was long ago. But why didn't they ask long ago?"

—Villiana Calac Hyde, Yumáyk Yumáyk

Hantak Siny: Frog Woman
By Theresa Gregor

Woman Warrior
Survivor
Redeemer

I must imagine
Her mind
Her voice
Her power
To bring forth
Death.

I must imagine
Her song
Her story
Her struggle
Her sacrifice.

Did she feel insecure?
Like a stranger in her own skin?
Did she feel threatened
From dangers, within
Her home, community?
Did she tell
Her mother, sister, aunt?

I must imagine
Her song
Her story
Her struggle
Her sacrifice.
Who heard her song?
Who believed her story?
Who supported her struggle?
Who sacrificed for her?

A dark sky signals
Rising moon on horizon
Remember her story?
Remember her struggle?

A lustful stare
Wandering eyes
Unwanted embrace
Groping hands
Upon her body.

Imagine
Her disgust
Wiyot's stare and his touch
Does it really matter what it was?
We all know what he wanted.

Imagine
There was more to her story
Before the Ancestors
Prepared for His death
There were other preparations.
A walk to gather medicine,
A cleansing bath, sage burned, teas made,
Prayers to heal,
Prayers for strength,
Prayers for justice
To make Her, Us, whole again.

Hantak siny
We know your story
We need your song
We share your struggle.
We continue to sacrifice
Hear our cries
Hear our cries
Hear our cries.

Nim Wetsip: Awakening to Motherhood
By Poyomi Thopishin (Jasmine Curlin)

When I nurse Nim Wetsip
my body is no longer a
sexual being
but an instrument being
used to pass life energy
from one body to the next,
like a vase holding water.

When he screams out for me
it awakens my body and
pours out the elixirs
that I drink
full of all the medicines
and nourishment that he is
asking for.

I say my body is not a sexual
being because up until I
gave birth to him
I had only experienced my
body in relation to what
comes before the child.
The first time my breasts
swelled with the essence of
motherhood,
my sexuality became
dormant,
as my body was healing
from being broken open to
release my adolescence in
the form of him.

I am no longer the little girl
playing in the river,
curious if I'm wearing too
much to swim or not enough
to cover up my purity.

Looking around at the
womanly bodies that I
couldn't wait to grow into...
looking at my mother
through the eyes of my son,
I feed him as he feeds me.

Nim Wetsip
By Poyomi McDarment
Digital Painting

Nim Wetsip: Awakening to Motherhood (Poem) and Nim Wetsip (Digital Painting) is a collaboration of poetry and art by Poyomi Thopishin (Jasmine Curlin) and Poyomi McDarment, Tule River Yokut descendants.

Náavut
By Nichole Vasquez-Sutter
Linocut Reduction Print

Náavut

By Nichole Vasquez-Sutter

Náavut,
A symbol
Of womanhood,
Of motherhood,
The vulnerable self
Protected by a
Coarse exterior
Dangerous, only to those
Unaware of how to penetrate
Her boundaries.
Always protecting
Herself
Her flowers,
Her fruit
Life-giving strength.
An oasis of life
In the bountiful desert.

Milkyway $ungáal

By Camaray Davalos

Her day/night duality lets the sun kiss her
(skin, eyes, mouth)
places that the moon knows well.
Fingers nimble, knowing with their eyes closed
where each piece of $óyla goes.
Thread it in, pull it out.
Breathing.
She is the first basket stitch
being woven through the layers of time.
The rhythm of her grandmother's coils reach concentrically
towards the edge of the universe.
Stars splash the upward walls,
reversing negative space.
Eyes the same color as manzanita,
as the plants she gathers to fill her basket and belly.
She loves that her skin is like
sun-dried juncus in the winter,
wet clay in the summer;
When she touches her skin,
it feels like home.
She has never felt more connected to the sky,
as when her feet dance atop the ground
at night, paths lit by firelight.
Strands of hair, thick with memory and longing
connect with the sky
stretching high, to the mercurian silver
that is the milky way.
Remembering takes place each time she sings a song.
Ancestors open their arms; they never ask what took so long.
And the stardust is their footsteps,
the comets are their spirits,
and their voices fill the
crevices of space,
you can hear it.

Túutuchivish – Free
Annalisa Berrios by Pekuna Hong, Native Hawaiian
Digital Photo

Photo taken during a retreat hosted by Native Hawaiian MMA fighter Llima MacFarlane and her foundation Nā Wahine Toa, which supports and empowers Indigenous women by teaching them how to defend themselves.

Great Oak
By Nichole Vasquez-Sutter

Dappled light over
Head, stems down through glowing oak leaves
Sharing the soft sky
With the firm earthen
Ground that our ancestors once
Walked upon before
Generations have
Passed under her boughs, giving
Life through nourishment
Squirrels climb through her leaves
Hiding acorns birthed from our
Mother Wi'áa$al

Unearthed
By Kelly Caballero

The cracks that were settled within my heart have erupted, blood pouring out
Irreparable, searing pain causing malfunction throughout the rest of my body
Hot globulus oceans escaping me
Catching momentum down the plains of my face
Meeting at the corners of my mouth like rivers, where escapes me, finally
Thoughts flooding my brain or drowning, I can't tell beyond this incessant ringing
Disoriented, destroyed, shutting down
Where bones once were, doubt took place
Crumbling to a floor that doesn't exist, nothing will catch me
Hands grasping for hope, clutching the space where my heart once was
Choking on the future I had dreamt
All that is left is skin, skin that resembles yours
Skin that kept me whole as continents within me shifted
Where my heart once was, a mountain is born
Treacherous and abandoned
A place where even love cannot survive

Kíicha
By Ericka Lopez
Graphite Pencil

Contact

By Megan Dorame

When the Spanish crossed over our river it was summer.
They stretched their arms out in front of their hearts,
and we met their beliefs first in the form of a framed portrait,
a painting of the Virgin herself.
Her cerulean sheath, specked with silver stars
and her sea-like eyes were of interest.
Pale men with similar eyes wore robes the color of our earth,
the color of what we crawled out of in our creation.
Was it the Virgin's brilliance
or her tears that lured us out of our homes
and down from the hills?
We brought our seeds and our shell money,
and we set them down.
When they poured water over our heads,
were we kneeling?

We did not know.

Kúp *(Sleep,Dormant)*

"Chó'on híicha yumáyk míiqu$. Polóov míiqu$. Pitóo híicha yáawaq."

"All these things existed a long time ago. It was good. Now they are gone."

—Villiana Calac Hyde, Yumáyk Yumáyk

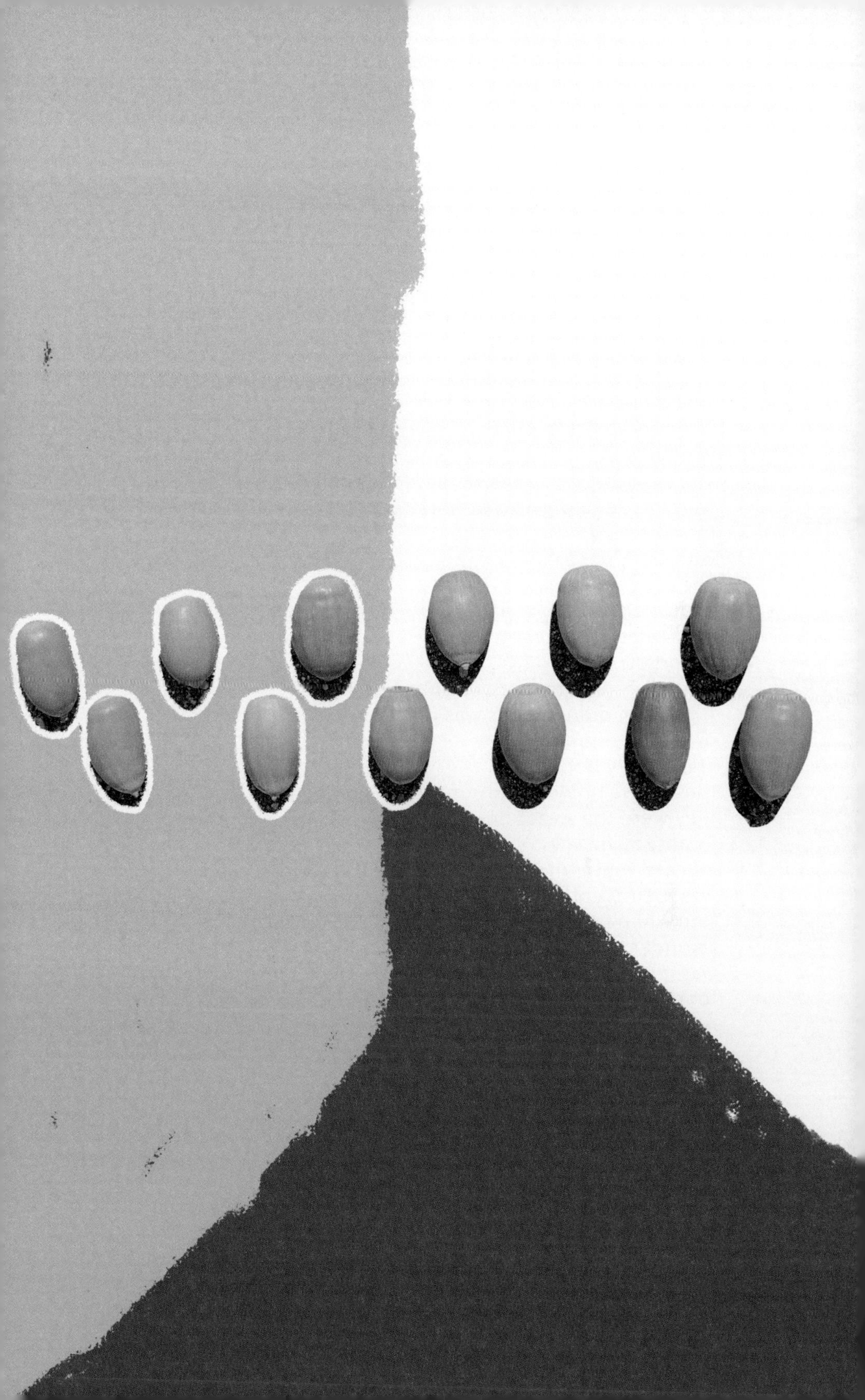

Sweet Orange

By Megan Dorame

When the sickness came,
it scudded over the old mission grounds, infecting,
snake-like and silent.
The survivors, the ones we descended from,
were few.
The survivors, the ones we descended from,
were made to dig a great hole.
Into the hole went the ones
who were not as lucky.
The hole filled fast,
and when it did, the padres,
they wanted to forget.
To forget,
a grove of orange trees was planted.
A grove of orange trees was planted
over a mass grave.
The history books say
these were not your run-of-the-mill oranges,
they were the sweet ones.
I want to know if,
on cold winter mornings, when the trees blossomed,
was their scent saccharine or stinking?
And when the trees bore fruit,
I wonder,
was it boiled down, and mixed with sugar
for marmalade? Did the padres spread it over bread?
And did they lick their lips after they bit into their breakfast?
What I really want to know is
if trees grew fruitfully,
fed by flesh,
or was their growth stunted
by the decomposition of a people?

Uncle
By Kaitra Sbragia

Uncle.

I've been staying busy to stall the heavy settling of realization that this distance is kindly hiding. These towns separating me from the reality that there is no longer a you, begin to recede when my heart rate drops; when my mind slows; when my feet stop. It pulls me so slightly, like the tide's workings on your toes in the sand. Out of my control sliding into the mind, no distance can match memory.
Your hair. Crash. Recede.
Your eyebrows, raised high in disgust. Crash. Recede.
The smile that beams. Crash.
So much so that it crinkles your nose. Recede.
And draws your shoulders up to your ears. Recede.
I am pulled by the currents. Crash. Recede.
I must move. Squelch as I pull the current captives from their space in the sand.
I run. I must. I run. Back into the sea, not away.
Until I pass the first break.

Thieved

By Emily Clarke

For all missing and murdered Native women.

i feel too slow
in my gut
when i am close
to losing my wholeness
(my womanness)

the taut skin of my back is branded
skin says:
INDIGENOUS
or
FOR YOUR TAKING
or
PLEASE FETISHIZE ME

i am a branded
woman
we are all burnt
women
the worst kind

a cousin who runs marathons
and sword fights gloom
is a branded woman too

an auntie who molds
tortillas and frybread in yellow oil
is a branded woman too

a sister who squanders green at the tiny casino
and spends nights with body splayed on earth
is a branded woman too

the same woman
the same women
all
always
and the same brand:
a murder
a rape
a man
a badge

women stolen,
not lost
(is there a point in calling myself a *not yet?*)
tribal survival rethought
(never rebuilt, never)
because the loss of
woman, is the loss of
heart: engorged,
warm

⅓ of murdered U.S. women are
INDIGENOUS
⅓ of murdered U.S. women are
INDIGENOUS
INDIGENOUS
INDIGENOUS
and loss has the power
to gobble culture
and loss has the power
to drown ritual in shadows
and loss has the power
to silence an entire people

To my Unborn
By Jenah Lattin

Where does your spirit belong now?
To whom does it belong?

Do you fly with the Golden Eagles?
The keepers of wisdom, transcendence of spirit.

Are you released into the wind?
Drifting towards the eternal sun.

Do you walk with the Buffalo herds?
The blessings of life, mothers of the sacred.

Or do you belong to the water?
Dissolving into the ocean of a thousand cosmos.

I saw you in my vision.
The center of life
'É' et ne 'áyu 'e Nená 'eqwe.

shapeshifter
By Emily Clarke

bones of ancestors
wind-chimed from trees
by the wrists, my
cheeks cherried thrice,
butchered in the bust,
belly bowl scraped
empty, left a rind,
filled with the clinking
of ghost bells, forced
to be an offering,
my heart-shaped offal
strung like my
predecessors, callous
grin, teeth filed down by
mother tongue, yes,
premonition does me well,
i remember my fostered
heart and the blood moon,
my eye not yet spade, i
remember the potent
lashings, my suture
unfastened, the sound
of sulfur escaping, i
remember the shaman
entering my skin, damp
fingers climbing my spine
like a rope, the
mud beneath the spring
opens like a door, pneuma
era threatening to flee, i
remember my descent.

Daddy Singing in the Shower
By Annalisa Berrios

Because he no longer
swallows liquid,
he stands alone under warm water
to chant our native song.
The water pounds on him as if
It were his father.

I sit hidden.

My heart beats faster as he sings louder.
Steam creeps from under the cracks
like a bad dream on a scary night.
My soul cries for a warrior
who does not know
that his oldest daughter can hear his sorrow.

His deep voice carries my faith
as I become his pain
slipping down the drain.

Tip-toeing away wanting to believe,
he knows eyes shed tears

and his daughter has the strength
to wipe them clear.

Best Picture
By Meadow Fuller

Their singing crashed through me. I couldn't translate the words. I didn't need to, it just was. In this, I'm beautiful.

my hair touches the floor, two braids that dust against the dirt that my ancestors walked.

I dance with them. My clothes, made by my grandma hang loosely around my body.

To my sweet rez,

I missed you like I missed myself. The beat skips, 1, 2, 2, 1, 2. Constantly, and without even realizing it. I catch the beat skip this time, I'm expecting it. How do I find my way back to you? The beat slows, exhaustive, asking, pleading, please Creator, please, we're tired. I'm so tired. We stop dancing. I angle my face toward the camera. A single tear drips down my face. They inhale. Beautiful, beautiful, the audience thinks. "This one will win the Oscar," someone whispers. From their hearts to God's feet. For once, I move with grace.

I fear that I never knew you.

Backwards
By Alexis Munoa Dyer

Grass worshippers. Farm disciples. Holiness
In the destruction of what is naturally occuring.
Mining. Cutting. Raking. Chopping.
Hacking at the branches of our ancestors.
Years of Mother's work gone in an instant.

The same violence on
my body.
Our missing.
Our murdered.
Our mothers.
I went to this place to speak with
My Grandmothers. I came to heal.
Instead this view intruding my prayers.

Supreme in "realities."
Domination a love language.
Imagining themselves separate.
Fences, paths, roads. Dividing, labeling, forging.
A pious plow and plunder. Destroying life to enjoy it.

Backwards
By Alexis Munoa Dyer
Pentax 645, Portra 400

Where Did it Begin?
By Amanda Nogales

A people once so humble and proud.
Defiled.
Tainted.
Left to the brink of extinction.
Leaving only ashes and pondering souls.
Too scared to speak, silence is taught.
Where a warrior's cry once echoed,
We hear tears of lost children left to wander the night.

Guided by false promises of salvation;
We teach old ways, yet forget tradition.
Enchanted by the spotlight.
Blinded by its true intention,
"Forget all you know and whence you came from."

Now dependent on a society that
Denies broken promises.
Cloaked in Rott.
Humanity stripped.
Families torn.
Our young misused and maltreated.

Learned behavior.
They grow to inflict all that fall after.
No medicine strong enough to cure.
No smoke thick enough to smudge away.
No song loud enough to drown out.

Living Thing
By Rebecca Macarro

I am trying to remember the sun
while I am entrenched in fog
Except instead of confusion
I only feel clarity
I figure when all else fails, grip your wheel and drive west

To the sea
The waves, larger than life,
will threaten to swallow you
You can run
Or perhaps let them
And before you know it you are pulled under
Until the bottom regurgitates you to the surface
And the current carries you
To the place we go when it's all over

We were not supposed to survive
So waste not your life
You can swim back to shore
Reborn
Knowing that tomorrow would be lonely without you
a life worth living
Is all they ever asked for
Create joy and radical change inside of what is meant to make us suffer
Or perhaps
Alchemize the suffering
If within our means
And know you can return to po$úunik
When you are ready

House of Obsidian

By Camaray Davalos

I.

We were forced to kneel before a cross
of rusted nails and painted blood.
And they made us pray for our health
so that we could birth less Heathens
and more Catholics.

But before they crossed the oceans
We were autonomous.
'atáaxum consciousness
And our ancestors were making potions
of plants,
of power,
of purpose.

We could cultivate life
or not,
knowing that the first breath is the threshold
between
Life and Death.

II.

I have to remind you that it was
white men in black robes who tried to claim the land
like it was my body
and my body like it was the land.
Maybe because we are both
rolling, resolute, rhythmic. Rebellious.

And it is white men in black suits who
say my choice is a sin
because subordination
is their sharpest blade.
I've learned to dull it with my teeth.

III.
In our legacy of apothecaries,
Wisdom has been muted.

The intimacy formed with root relatives,

Muted.

The peace we allowed ourselves to have,
knowing our bodies are in our hands,

Muted.

But.
I still allow myself to walk through liminal spaces,
to befriend ancient knowledge.
Not because I was given permission
but because my being requires it.

IV.
The freedom to choose exists in ourselves,
not in books penned by men,
or the jealousness of gods.

That is why settler philosophies fall around me
like defective shells.
The antithesis of our obsidian-charged bodies;
Corroded, obsolete.
They do not work on us
because I am the master of this house
made of memories and stars from where we began.

And I love to disrupt unwanted guests' plans.

Wólnish *(Cultivate)*

"Xíl-uk puyáamangay. Pá' pí' champoróvori wóluk 'áyáalinik. Pó' yawáywish míiqu$."

"It would always rain. And our garden would grow just right. It was beautiful."

—Villiana Calac Hyde, Yumáyk Yumáyk

The Rez
By Nichole Vasquez-Sutter

Little feet crunch on
Spiky oak leaves strewn across
The cool path below

Walking among the
Sage, sunflowers and tall grass,
Squirrels and rattlesnakes,

Quiet and content,
I wait for the time when my
Cousins will arrive

At my grandpa's house
A trailer nestled among
The oak savannah

On the dusty Rez,
My family gathers around.
Memories of home.

1995

By April Bouchard

I span the distance between two points far too often.
The line has end points that I've defined as logical, yet meaningful emotions: love and passion.
The road between the two points is long and rough, but to me it's only zero time. Time I don't count as reality. Static.
Static until the station clears and music begins.
Each destination/departure point is equal. Each one holding a part of me that can't be exchanged or traded. Home, my love and my heart, could never assimilate to my life here.
Here is filled with a passion for the beauty that the world has to offer.
A passion that burns so purely and brightly inside of me, that I glow from within — I am like nothing they've seen, and cannot be contained. I am untouchable here,
not because I am fragile,
Because I am fierce. Here.
It's as if I've split myself in two.
Each half, although carrying the essence of one, live and breathe as separate entities.
Each one with different actions, emotions and personalities.
So how could these halves, two people, the two "me's", who are completely different,
Ever be loved by the same people? Accepted by the same people?
They, my love and my passion, are the two ends and I am the connecting line.
And only I walk this line,
Draw this line
And cross this line.
It's the length of my spirit.
And with such ends, it will never grow too thin.

Does My Shell Fit Your Idea of a Soul

By Meadow Fuller

I have a recurring dream, where my grandma grabs my two braids that scrape against the floor, and cuts them, right at their root. "You dirty girl," she snarls, "you really thought you were Indian?" I cry and I cry on the floor until my tears become redundant, and pick myself up, hardened on the inside.

She was right, I hadn't been **Indian** for a long time. Since I stopped checking Native and put Black instead. Or maybe it was when people started telling me I don't look like my mom.

The dream feels so real though. I think I want it to be. I can smell the banuelos, cooking in the background. *They're burning*, I think. Yeah, they're definitely burning. *The beans too*, she'll have a hard time scraping them off the bottom of the pot. I'll help her with that later.

Her hardened hands delivered me to the train of indigeneity. Our collective brokenness carries us forward. Look out the window, they've made dream catchers out of our complacency, moccasins out of our foolishness, and drums out of our inhibitions. Do you think they'll mind if I ask to borrow the Pocahontas costume they've made out of my own romantic words? I think I'll need it, when people look me in the eye.

With this new truth, I become an INDIGENOUS WARRIOR. STRONG RESILIENT INDIGENOUS. I AM HERE BECAUSE OF MY ANCESTOR'S PRAYERS. REZPECT YOUR ELDERS. **N** ATIVES **W** ITH **A** TTITUDE. Not the fake Indian I was before.

White people ask me where I'm from. PECHANGA. Surprise.

I WENT TO AN ELEMENTARY SCHOOL WITH ALL PECHANGA KIDS WHERE WE LEARNED OUR NATIVE LANGUAGE, I DON'T SPEAK LUISENO THOUGH, BUT ONE DAY I WILL AND I BASICALLY SPENT ALL MY TIME ON THE REZ AND I DANCE TRADITIONAL AND I WAS ON TRIBAL COUNCIL. They look at me with awe.

I've heard them call me all kinds of things. The *per cap* Indian, the *mystical* Indian, the *beautiful* Indian, the *black* Indian, the *lonely* Indian, the *cruel* Indian, the *destructive* Indian, the *destroyed* Indian. So it's okay when I scream those words from the bottom of my feet, when I sell a piece of my soul, my dignity, turn my head away from those who love me so I can stare at the sun some more, because since that day in my Abuela's kitchen, no one has ever called me a fake Indian.

We Do Have Seasons
By Rebecca Macarro

I sat atop the canyons
Just me on a bench carved to its death
Covered in lovers' names and tags
I came to watch the horizon burn
Bursting into hues of rust, lilac and gray,
with the night sky spilling into the supernova
like ink
The city lights below glittered in scattered groupings as if
they were mirroring the constellations obscured by clouds
and smoke
Millions of tiny particles swirled around me,
Both seen and unseen
ash and dust
carrying the aromas
Of bay laurel and sage
The Santa Anas always arrive as a shock to the system
yet always on time
When you are ready
You anticipate them
Initiating a hard reset and igniting the chaparral with second
chances
Whipping through the corridors of the elite on the west side,
and sweeping clear the streets of the east side
The winds have no class preference
In fact, they are more than just a weather phenomenon
My heart is open
My mind is clear
And I can say without a doubt
The winds are spirits
Here to rustle up the scorched brush and relieve the trees of
their fruit
To cool off from this long ass summer
To charge the ether with frequencies untapped by the numb
and mindless commuters and influencers
And make them wonder if they are losing their minds or is
there more to this place after all?
The winds lift the veil to awaken the dead and they dance
along the tectonic plates beneath us
together they glide across 12 miles or so

Revealing secrets, unearthing traumas,
shifting consciousness
Nothing in this place is ever settled
The sun has gone over the edge of the pacific
And having left my perch I now stand bearing witness to the
tumult of the gusty evening
At the intersection of fountain and sunset
Trees suffocated by planters
lay in state
palm fronds fly over the crosswalks
as if they have somewhere to be
Yesterday's newspaper lines the gutters and
parking citations litter the sidewalks
The air is humming with electricity
The algorithms that lead our lives are reprogrammed to
withstand the dark days ahead
I am not afraid of ghosts
So I lean into the winds and listen
They tell me,
"These are not your homelands, you cannot be a guest
forever...
The mountains that weep are calling you."
Not what I wanted to hear
I hope they show me the way back
I have been known to wander

Every Lover is a Warrior
By Jenah Lattin

Every lover is a warrior for the ones we refuse to lose.
Only through suffering can we remain humble.
The wounds inflicted and the fire that bled. The pain of
Rebirth arising from the ashes. The re-envisioning of life's
purpose, steady and true.
Bound to the world, prisoner of my own restraints.
The slow burn of numbing pain,
The deep pain of my mother, my sisters, my ancestors
for our men that lose themselves in the fire.
My spirit aching for release, no longer bound to
the burden we carry.
Far away into the wind
I must go for awhile.

Missing Piece
By Desiree Wetz

I have heard of old things
I have wondered where they have gone
Surely, they could not have all disappeared
I have seen those that have something trailing behind them
Others cannot see them
They don't see and feel what I have
But I cannot ignore it
And that scares me greatly
I fear that I do not understand what is wanted
But I will try.

How Do You Pronounce It?
By Avelaka Macarro

"How do you pronounce it?"
"So is that Russian?"
"What does it mean?"
"Where does it come from?"
"Do you live on the reservation?"
"I didn't know Indians still existed..."

Avelakayawaywish Marcyna Aquino Macarro
Avelaka- əvɛlɑkʌ
36 letters. 4 names. 1 girl.

I have been asked a million questions for each name, the total of which describes each part of my ancestral existence, both past and present. Names do not predict a person's future any more than a tarot set or a weather forecast. They are aspirational at best, a hope for the child in a legal space. The meanings are personal to the parents, even if the child forgets their name is more than a calling card.

This is the fate of most names, but it was never mine. I've been trapped with questions of meaning and origin, pronunciation and spelling. I thought my name was a plague when I was younger, slowly invading the spaces of foreign strangers. In a sea of Katelyn/Caitlyn/Kaitlinns, Sara(h)s, and Hannahs, I was already different.

My nominal existence made me crave normality, especially when the already typical girls proved that homogeneity was important. Maybe I could be "Elizabeth" or simply "Belle" in respect to my media heroines who were personably different, and still accepted by the end of their stories. Maybe I could be accepted as a person and not a name.

I slowly turned my name into a joke by responding to various degradations — not just in the mispronunciation, but in nicknames. Peers remembered how to spell "Avelaka" by creating Avenue Laka (Ave.Laka) and ridiculed its fullness (Avelakayawaywish) with the witty "Avelaka yo I WISH I had a different name". My daily routine already included an exhausting guessing game, but I was willing to further lose myself to my predominantly white classmates. By 4th grade I was painfully aware of the structural issues of my name (was Yawaywish a middle name?) and the documental challenges my identity produced (standardized testing is rarely friendly to long, atypical names). "Avelaka" was owned by the people and papers I interacted with, and I became more aware with that as I continued socializing outside my family.

My name became a precursor to who I was as an individual. I couldn't gloss over my calling card. The implacability of my name is part of historical genocide. My tribal language is considered dead, saved by modern academics and a rez school, but still untenable for the majority of the population. Even my name betrays the truth of the language. It's supposed to be Avellakayawaywish Mukara, but the two parts were molded to fit a world of racism and partially limit nominal explanations.

Avelaka prevents total bastardization in spelling and pronunciation, though it is equally a reduction of the native truth. Mukara was similarly strained over two generations to enforce Mexican imagery and remove the layer of serfdom imposed on Indigenous persons. Although my name was an action against this (I am the oldest person with a Luiseño name), its authenticity was forced apart on legal terms: Avelaka is acceptable, Avelakayawaywish is not.
This is the government's continued removal of nativeness to digestible terms. The roots of the reservation come from a similar shortening, from the expanse of the continent to a square block.

With every register, classroom, and position I took on, "Vel" assumed the role of my calling card. It was too exhausting to reintroduce myself, with my name, its pronunciation, followed by practiced commentary. My nicknames became nom de guerres — my personal war with normalcy, invisibility, and ancestry. I reworked my title repeatedly: "Vel" for everyday conversation; "Belle" for Starbucks and restaurant reservations; "Mariposa" arrived in Argentina; and "Ave" continued my joke existence. I thought I was protecting myself and my privacy, and I cannot tell if I am wrong to do so.

My real name thus becomes an audible prayer: hoping it is said correctly and recited to others with more fervor than the rosary. I can see the second someone hears my name. They follow each syllable with confusion, turning each letter with dyslexic focus, rummaging through their catalogue of common words, and silently asking me to repeat, slower, please. And I do, rephrasing the information with personal disgust and seasoned patience. As each person attempts to recite the rarity, I am quick to say it again (only this time with a smile). The anger I feel in this dance is not with the other speakers, it is with me and the forgotten language I carry every day. Foreign tongues cannot be blamed when they awkwardly taste the steely syllables of my ancestral blood.

My name should float through conversation like an actual butterfly: delicately, but reflective of the up and down movements. When compared to other Luiseño words, Avelaka easily transcends the cultural norms of Anglo-American names with the grounded challenge of my tribal language. Yawaywish feels more natural and familiar to an Indigenous speaker, beautiful in pronunciation and tangible in its authenticity. Perhaps this is why I feel ashamed when I drop it from my character. I not only lose the name, I lose my mother tongue.

Because my birth certificate never allowed the two parts of my first name to stay together, I don't identify with Yawaywish. As far as I knew, Yawaywish was a silent name, reflected only in my display of indigeneity and invisible in my total sum. I chose Marcyna as the sole middle name because it felt personal and easy. It wasn't bombarded by questions because it sounded so similar to other popular names (Marcy/Martha). I could decide when and where to explain it (it is the name of a fictional princess in the 1950s musical Kismet). It is exotic, but in a shallow, joyous way. More of a fun fact than a lesson in historical trauma.

Whenever I was forced to address my full name, Yawaywish became a lie. No one calls me Avelakayawaywish because yawaywish is descriptive, not actual. Avelaka alone says more about my personality and transitory nature. Part of evaluating my name comes from accepting Yawaywish in the

"Avelaka Explanations"; I have to say it to tell the whole story. I don't hate it because I'm done hating my name. I prefer now to indulge in its strangeness, the many y's and a's that return levity to an otherwise dead word. Even the last part, the "wish", feels like a reconciliation for my native language, my chamtéela, like my forefathers placed an exclamation point on our Indigenous legacy.

I am not sure if I fulfilled the dream by existing or if I betrayed it by relying on the languages of colonizers. I still respond to Belle and Bella with more readiness than Yawaywish, something I can only unlearn if its meaning is taught. I stand now in favor of full name introductions. In favor of teaching the unknown native history. In practicing patience with the móomyam and refusing shortened names and mispronunciation. My diction will become clearer and more certain as I hold the future of chamtéela on my driver's license, passport, and coffee orders. As my tribe reclaims its name, now the repossessed Payómkawichum, so do I. Not just Avelaka or Ave or Vel, but Avelakayawaywish.

Bird Songs
By Megan Dorame

In our piousness, we once sea-bathed before sunrise;
were we ever clean. We danced like water birds
our arms outstretched, wings.
Feathers plumed, we reflected the light.
We cocked our heads, tucked our wings back and ducked
before rising again,
slower than time, timeless.
Deliberate, breath-like movements,
defying laws and gravity itself: bird steps.

When we lost our steps with the dusk,
with the darkness,
we could not help it. Daylight always comes,
and when it does, we search.
My own steps often tread much too heavy.
My feet are tired,
and so too, is the ground.
I stretch and strain, searching, always searching
for steps that move, bird-like;
I have not found that grace yet.

Rebirthed
By Kelly Caballero

One year later
Under a sun that has been cloaked in black
A tiny sky-blue blossom emerges from
the dust of a broken heart
Her battle cry is existence
This humbled resistance!
I bow to her, chin to chest
It was the warm touch of memory
The gold lining of a sun cloaked in black
Feeding the soils of transformation
My offerings of flesh and tears fed and watered this evolution
Creating a homeland for this love
that survived my fervent will not to
Tiny sky-blue blossom, all that I have...
A seed of defiance, who arose alone dancing under molte despair
Singing of acceptance and reassurance that death does not mean
an end
But the melody of love succeeds all and life begins again.

Living as an Indigenous Woman
By Makayla Murillo

I see Morro Hills, where our creation story began. I walk through San Luis Rey Mission, where our ancestors walked. This is our home, and our people's home. As a descendant of the San Luis Rey Band of Luiseño Indians, my Indigenous world views and embracing my culture has led to a career of working with Native communities and tribal lands.

My devotion for Mother Earth and my community has stemmed from my Native heritage, encouraging me to participate as an Indigenous woman to understand more about cultural resource management and archaeology. My perspective towards Cultural Resource Management (CRM) is a tired one; the stigma associated with archaeology, the challenges of being an Indigenous woman on the field, and cultural beliefs do not make for a simple life in archaeology, but for a rewarding one.

I am the eyes and voice for Indigenous tribes during all phases of development. I am employed with an environmental firm as an archaeologist, working alongside various tribes in southern California, advancing relationships amongst each other to help preserve and protect our sacred sites. My goal is to be a top Native female archaeologist, while uniting natives and archaeologists on the field.

The knowledge I have gained has resulted from having a career as both a Native representative for a tribal company as well as being an archaeologist. Both careers have taught me balance between science and culture. The stigma within archeology is that archaeologists are disrespectful to sacred lands and resources. We are often thought of as "grave robbers": accused of disturbing Indigenous burial grounds and resurfacing sacred resources that are meant to stay in place. As an Indigenous woman, I come with the respect and knowledge of tribal resources. As an archaeologist, I handle valuable resources with care. The true disturbers are the development companies that capitalize and exploit our land. Archaeologists record, collect, and excavate to prevent and mitigate any negative impacts near sites. Tribes within the project location are contacted for further education on sites.

We monitor every phase of the project to protect any and all cultural resources and sites. Recommendations are given to development companies to avoid and protect ancestral spaces.

I have discovered many challenges with being an Indigenous female archaeologist. Discussing my Native background with non-Natives and sharing with my Indigenous community that I'm an archaeologist has been troublesome. So, I developed my own balance. When I'm the only Indigenous woman on the field surrounded by predominantly white males, I have to speak loudly for my concerns. As a member of a hugely marginalized minority group, it is my responsibility to voice my concerns and opinions at difficult times. With these challenges, I am eager to begin building bridges between Native communities and non-Native archaeologists; we both want to preserve and protect.

My passion for archeology and science will never interfere with my culture or beliefs. Always, I carry protection wherever I go; sage in my tool box and prayers from the heart. My elders have taught me the importance of ritual at sacred sites. We have necessity and passion to preserve our land and remind the country that we are still here. We have been here all along. My goal is to change the way our society portrays the Native community and protect our only Earth. Even with the criticism I have had in my career, I will never stop fighting for my ancestors, community, or future generations. As an indigenous woman, I am obligated to support, fortify, and protect our Native communities, land, and resources.

To My Children
By Alexis Munoa Dyer

Nokáamay
You bright eyed chixémal
A voice of crystal clear laughter
No$wáamay
You brilliant sparkling alóomax
A heart of passion and wonder
You are the reason Tútu held on
You are the breath of the mothers
You are the words we speak to The Earth
No$úun Lóoviq that we have each other.

Nokáamay
By Alexis Munoa Dyer
Pentax 645, Ilford HP5

'Óomay ló'xakat néy – My Ancestors Made Me
By Casse Kihúut
Digital Painting

To My Sister
By Genevra Munoa

As the waves embrace
So does she
As the light reflects
Bending colors into beauty
So does she
As the stars expand never ending
possibilty
So does she
As the air gives and moves and frees
So does she
As the sand holds on to me
So does she

$ó'a *(Bloom)*

"Qáy míikinga cháam yú'pan 'á$únnga némaxkutum, qáy...Pí cháam móliqa."

"We're never going to go back to that again, no, never...But we remember."

—***Villiana Calac Hyde, Yumáyk Yumáyk***

Probable Imagination

By Meadow Fuller

I leave juncus in the bathrooms
And deergrass in the classrooms
It makes me feel less lonely
To know I'm not the only Indian here.
The only Indian at the Number One Public University
Not the only one I know,
But I've met the other ones, and they didn't like me.
I think they thought I was weird.
I wore my special beaded earrings only around them,
But I just looked like a Halloween costume

I wanted to thank my basket,
For holding my secrets,
Holding my Luiseño,
And being kind to me.
Without you, I would've dropped out by now
I envisioned how it would go, relentlessly
I would've looked at everyone's faces, and known that none of them were mine,
I would've carried my things in a kúnla thrown over my shoulder
No
I just would've carried you in that sack.
You deserve that respect.

All of my other things can stay, they're tainted now.
So barefoot, all the way home.
I've grown out of all my shoes anyways.
Maybe when I get there we can sing songs to each other
I knew that you were singing songs to me,
When I didn't want to listen
When looking at you made me hate my being,
When I thought how stupid it was to be Indian,
How much easier it would be if I let it go
The pale men in the expensive suits stand in the front and tell me that
Race is just a social construct
That I constructed this suffering and I could deconstruct it if I wanted to.
I stopped being Indian for a while
I thought it helped
But every race gets lonely, even the white people.
And being lonely in Indian sounds more poetic than being lonely in white.
I think instead of a song, we could just lay on the ground,
Even if it's the cold tile,
Or the dirt where a thousand red ants bite me
Saying hello, and welcoming me home.

'Atáaxum

By Nichole Vasquez-Sutter

Our existence is
Persistence as we journey
Honoring all of
Our ancestors
People of the West, we strive
As one family
Payómkawichum,
Decolonized minds speak free
Chamchá' 'ahíkya.

STRENGTH IS WOVEN INTO HER DNA.

Strength is Woven into her DNA
By Marlene' Dusek
Photography, DSLR Camera Photoshop, Lightroom
Pictured weaving: Monae Salgado (Cahuilla, Payómkawish)

Indigenous Motherhood

By Tristen Orosco

Love. What is love to you? What does it look like? How do you communicate the love for someone or something? Can you even put into words the feeling of love? Sure, I love my family and friends. I love my culture and where I come from, the land along with the animals and plants. I love and loved these things my entire life, it's all I knew. There is however a different type of love, a special sacred love between a mother and her children. It's hard to put into words this type of love. A special bond is formed throughout the ten months of pregnancy. For those ten months the mother and child are one, sharing everything. At birth they work together so that the new soul can finally be Earth side. You may think that this combined entity ends at birth but, it doesn't. For months this bond and love grows deeper and deeper as a mother nurses her infant. The bond is sacred. One cannot survive without the other.

The birth of my son brought a love that cannot be described. I would do anything and everything to protect him. Yes this is the "Mama Bear" in me but, it's more than that. We were and are one, for now. In those ten months of pregnancy I was never alone, I always had my baby with me. I'd talk to them and tell them stories. Stories I made up, stories about my life and their father's life, and stories that have been passed down from generation to generation. They were with me when I laughed and when I cried.

With this love comes tons of hope and also a lot of anxiety. While I was in college I learned about Indigenous women and children being targeted because they carry the culture. Indigenous women ensure that their culture and people will survive. They are the cultural carriers, thus targeted. I am a cultural carrier. This means it is my responsibility to teach and guide my son in cultural practices.

What does this even look like? To me, this means speaking chamtèela to him, even if it's basic phrases. This means cooking Indigenous foods, taking him to traditional gatherings, learning about Native plants, and so much more. I often lay awake late at night, not because he's awake, but because my mind is racing on how I am going to make sure my son can navigate this world without feeling like he's living in two different worlds.

I have often heard Native youth talk about this, I even talked about this; living in two different worlds. You're Native, trying to establish an identity that's traditional but, there are also all these outside modern distractions. You need a job and money and are influenced by social media and technology. In addition, we live in a world where people of color are targeted with hardly any justice served. Patriarchy fills not just society but, sometimes our own community. There also is a disconnect between youth and adults where one is seen as inferior and the other superior. It is a rough and confusing world to navigate as these are things that are not a part of our traditional culture.

Two years ago I was in Standing Rock protesting the Dakota Access Pipeline. While I was there, I remember listening to elders say the youth of today are becoming smarter than those in society. Why? Because the youth have learned to be strong in their identity while also understanding today's modern world and how it works. This is what calms me from going down the rabbit hole on those nights I lay awake thinking. My son will have a strong Payómkawichum and Lakota identity and he will understand how our modern world works. He is a glimmer of hope in a world that seems so backwards at times. He is what our ancestors prayed for—that our people and culture will continue. That love will continue.

Beyond Loss
By Avelaka Macarro

I didn't know what to think, and (even worse) I didn't know what to do.

When my dad told me my brother had passed, I crumpled to the floor. The weight of worry had finally crushed me to a point of no return. I spent so much time thinking about the trauma that my ancestors endured, the struggles that followed them, but I always assumed my experience with that trauma was in the past tense. I didn't understand that every part of that trauma experience was still active. It was in my blood, dictating all my motivations. It was in every compassionate glance to my students, the way I defended my work, and especially in the way that I cared for my family. My life, my sorrow, all of it was centered around the histories of my ancestors. My tears were suddenly a flood built over hundreds of years.

It's one of the compelling parts of being a person of color, of being Indigenous, of being a minority within a minority. In a tribe that has only a few thousand people, it's hard to imagine that your experience isn't unique. But it's been repeated in old westerns, Buffy Saint-Marie songs, Sherman Alexie books, in the words of the other women in this book, all of whom know the constant beat of sorrow. It's burrowed deep on our reservations and in those who were kept away from their homeland. What I wish for myself—the future me, the past me, and the person who's been broken for a little over a year—is to respect the pain. To respect what it could teach me. What I thought was escapable, was in fact part of my DNA.

When my brother joined our ancestors, he left the piece of himself that couldn't be forgotten. The part that made us care about ourselves, and forced us to care about each other. His death summoned my most hidden thoughts of loss, not just the literal absence. His death was sudden, it was painful, and it was unnecessary. But in the pain, his death also brought me closer and gave me a new understanding of my Payómkawichum. It's in the traditions that we know who we are.

As Indigenous people, we've known loss intimately for hundreds of years, and have had to reckon with and reclaim the absence of our people, our sacred places, even the words that kept us connected to each other. We've known loss with an intensity that it's become one of the most certain traditions we hold. The songs, the rituals, even the land where we bury ourselves become the focal point of our civilization. It's no surprise that the only respect for our land comes when old bones and fragmented objects are found. When death becomes the only constant practice, it can feel like the most tethered part of our culture.

In my brother's words, "death is the one thing we know to be true". It's where tradition is remembered and practiced, where every person's body and life is given respect. In these traditions and songs, we were able to escape the defamation of the Catholic Church and the United States government. It's where we remind ourselves to hug our loved ones. It reminds us to come home to the land our ancestors, elders, and elders-in-training continue to defend. When I think seven generations ahead, I know I will not be here, but that my passing will provide a teaching and a reason to return to this land.

At the burning of my brother's belongings, I watched my cousins and family friends dance to the Nukwáanish songs that I had never heard, and I was reminded that there is more to learn about my people. And in their absence, I'm so grateful for my relatives, my ancestors, for existing in the first place.

Our Future
By Desiree Wetz

My heart is weary
My people have to change to exist in this future
Yet we try to hold onto the past
Traditions forgotten
Beliefs laid to rest
It wouldn’t be fair to forget what our ancestors endured
Even if it’s too easy to forget
It is by sheer will that we are still here
Our children must know the past
It helps them look out for a better future.

Cogstones/The Pleiades

By Megan Dorame

My looted

heritage

entombed in walls

and glass and

meticulously

numbered and

displayed for all to

see:

Like it is theirs and

like it was never

meant to live

in sky

or ground.

Stars made of stones are housed only

a mile away.

I feel their pulse so I steal them. Stars made of stones

I throw them back into sky,

giving them back to

the night.

She Peers Into the Collective Spirit of the Universe
By Jenah Lattin

She peers into the collective spirit of the universe
Listening to its secrets in the waves.
She surfs the moonlit ocean, chasing the midnight sunset.
Her feet touch the ground, but the sky can't contain her spirit.
Eagle calls to her, connecting between two hearts
To the expanding knowledge of wisdom,
Set free in the wind.
If the moon holds her secrets,
The Sun throws them back to the stars,
So that he could see her at least once more.

Notóowi 'ahétha'ax – My Open Spirit

Annalisa Berrios by Pekuna Hong, Native Hawaiian

Digital Photo

Photo taken during a retreat hosted by Native Hawaiian MMA fighter Llima MacFarlane and her foundation Nā Wahine Toa, which supports and empowers Indigenous women by teaching them how to defend themselves.

Curative Creativity: The Power of Cooking as Healing

By Camaray Davalos

I am blanching ivory-colored yucca blossoms, once, twice, thrice: a lengthy process, but necessary to take away the bitterness of the plant. I've taken on a culinary task I've never taken on before...Maybe because I never had time, until now. In the background, Donna Summer sings liquid melodies, reminding me to step sweetly, twirl, and dip as I tend the blossoms in the boiling cauldron. Time is something I don't mind taking. Lately, I've found this idea manifests itself most strongly when I'm working with food. That's why I find myself allowing the blanching to take as long as it needs to. I patiently wait and welcome the leisurely turning of the water from clear to gold, signifying the chemical process of this California native plant becoming more and more edible.

Now more than ever, I feel it's my responsibility as a descendant of Indigneous people of Southern California to tap into the traditions and creative processes my ancestors did hundreds, if not thousands, of years ago. Our people are Payómkawichum, 'People of the West'. Our climate is warm, sometimes unbearably so, yet it yields plenty of biodiversity in the form of edible plants. Our language is long, drawn out, and so are our ways of doing things: from cultivating, gathering and processing plants, to turning them into culinary creations.

I think back to the day before, when my partner and I found and gathered this yucca, and I remember how intimately tied I am to it; the way we touched feet to earth as we searched the chaparral for the freshly blooming stalk, as my ancestors must have as well; the way I peeled off each blossom, careful to leave alone the part where a silvery spider spun their web; the way I carefully inspect each petal for tiny insects. This must be slow food, an idea I had always admired from afar, but never quite had the time to adopt into my life. The idea that food should be grown and harvested locally, and take time to be prepared is a beautiful sentiment, but one that I, with meetings and work and schedules, had not allowed myself to become familiar with.

I came with that same slow energy when I was making a bowl for lunch with another native California specialty: Claytonia perfoliata, or in our native language, 'tóowish po páaku'. They remind me of lily pads, with a tiny white flower nestled in the center. This viridescent, broadleaf plant is nutrient dense, filled with Vitamin C. My bowl consisted of many layers: jasmine rice, a roasted black bean patty, baked eggplant slices, and hummus. To finish, I finely chopped the greens, careful to not apply too much pressure, and tenderly placed them on top of the bowl. The greens adorned the dish like a springtime crown, or a freshly picked bouquet.

Who was I, as I took a step back to admire this creation? Rarely did I take this time making lunch for only myself, and how bold of me to actually enjoy making it, like I had created a piece of art. I think this ancestral energy has always been here, though latent. It reminds me to take it slow, especially during a time when everything is so uncertain with the ongoing pandemic. There is therapy in the preparation of plants as food, as every component is mindfully gathered, curated, and spoken to, from start to finish. It was then I realized that I don't want preparing my food, especially our traditional foods, to be something that's a bedrudging task; I need it to be the part of my life that sustains my body and my soul. And I need to reconnect to being mindful about my food; too often I mindlessly consume, not paying much attention to the way faster food affects my health. I want to carry this appreciation for the small joys of food preparation into the future with me; the careful sorting of plants gathered by hand; the mundane tasks of blanching and waiting; and the art of delicately arranging greens from the land onto a dish. It is all healing.

Regeneration
By Marlene' Dusek

Take me to the lands where the chapparal, oak woodlands,
prairies, and the forest understory are burned in a traditional
cycle.

The lands during springtime yúulalash, deergrass, and many
other plant ancestors regenerate from kút, fire, in the fall.
The lands where my ancestor's DNA remains after managing
for generations.

Túutu, grandmother, told me that to have strong materials
for your basket, you must pray, sing, and manage with kút.

I was hoping you could take me to the lands where the oaks
are healthy, and the acorns are bug-free.
The lands where the seeds need kút to germinate.

The lands where kút has nourished tamáayawut's,
earthmother's, soils, where water cycles thrive.

Notice how I don't say "wildfire". That's a different concept
you see.

Our 'atáaxum have a word, 'akúumisa, meaning exposed to
fire and smoke for too long, or a wildfire, a high-intensity fire,
more detrimental than the kút I speak of.
Wildfire hit these lands with colonizers starting in 1542.

Genocide, forceful removal, harmful practices on the lands,
and outlawing of cultural traditions came with different
phases of colonization committed by Europeans, Spanish
mission systems, Mexican ranchos, and gold miners.

After this, most of the lands that were kút adapted became
grazing lands for cattle and livestock.
Overgrazing caused more and more destruction, and the
spread of seed that was alien to this ecosystem.

During California's first year of statehood in 1850 came

criminalization for cultural practices that had been carried out on these lands for millennia. The 1945 policies of suppression of kút continued. Maybe you are familiar with Smokey the Bear, the fire suppression propaganda that's lasted for 70+ years?

The chaparral got thicker, the forest understory became crowded. Dangerous levels of fuel were built and different managing styles are now on lands so broken up and divided;

consequences our elders told us would come from constant extraction and mistreatment of tamáayawut.

WILDFIRE: APPARENT DEVASTATION.

I say kút not to scare you, but to remind you that

This relationship is an old one,
A natural one.

Regeneration of many cycles are dependent upon
kút for existence.
Our peoples have always been in tune with this.

The lands that I speak of are right here.
We must repair this balance, this way of living.

We must regenerate with kút.

Perception through Reflection

By Emily Burgueno

Reflecting through beginnings,
Twenty seven years present but, reaching out beyond to where I descend which retains my return
Sharing this being as anything other than ceremony would dishonor all my mother surrendered
and ancestors survived to ensure each experience
Physically starting with a prayer between my mother and father
You know that prayer that you can hardly find within yourself when that's your only option?
A prayer they didn't know they needed
A healing she chose to welcome breaking down intergenerational cycles burning ceremonies since invasions
Rooted in umbilical cord beginnings, ones that stem from creation
This is why they tell us raising Kumeyaay babies are part of our ceremony
They bring the balance of creation
Constantly trying to retain my flow of offerings and sacrifice through ancestral veins and arteries
Keeping a connective balance of creation from past to present
It can sound something like your Great Gram's prayers but, spoken by your baby niece
An empowering purified nutrient healing even the most traumatic cycles
Continuing this ceremony within this constant second world pull, I link ancestral veins and arteries to guide each commitment
It can look like when my people gathered in an area
they descend from yet have been absent into decades of dehumanization

Still today continually displayed in ways that have systematically erased our presence
Hearing echoes of chee'yo in halls of pain, activating those ancient flows cut off at our life source
It can taste grainy or smooth like sha'wii
Each tasteful grain you can almost feel the process that Papa and Grams took their time guiding us kids with
Straining the bitterness away, leaving just a bit to keep you humble
If you cook it real good, you begin to taste the strength from each generation
Acknowledging ku'palth's seasonal sacrifice
Closest veins to her creation and she selflessly offers it
Connecting her creation with rezpect through the generations
Smelling as strong as the fire smoke that stays with us after leaving each sacred flame
Traces of oak on my clothes reminds me the importance of each song
It reminds me huta'pah is not far
Continually teaching by showing us how not to be
It can feel like 3 a.m. when your body is telling you to rest
Reminders of creation sung to enter your heart
Telling us to WAKE UP
Be present for the people
Continue together, for each other
These perceptions of my reflection into this ceremony ignite understandings to my flame
Yáayahun for days and nights it burns bright warming not just my ceremony but those around me
Yáayahun for times I lose myself in that second world and can't seem to translate my purpose
For I can only find that translation in creation
Reflection doesn't start with me, it begins with creation

Moloka'i

By Kaitra Sbragia

Just yesterday I thought I would die here.
Me, brown, among the red clay,
The green leaves, the blue sea.
Here they would search for me. My remnants.
Their remembrances.
I am the sea foam, white. I am the colors. One
Flash and we merged. Into one. White.

Néy – Self Portrait
By Casse Kihúut
Digital Painting

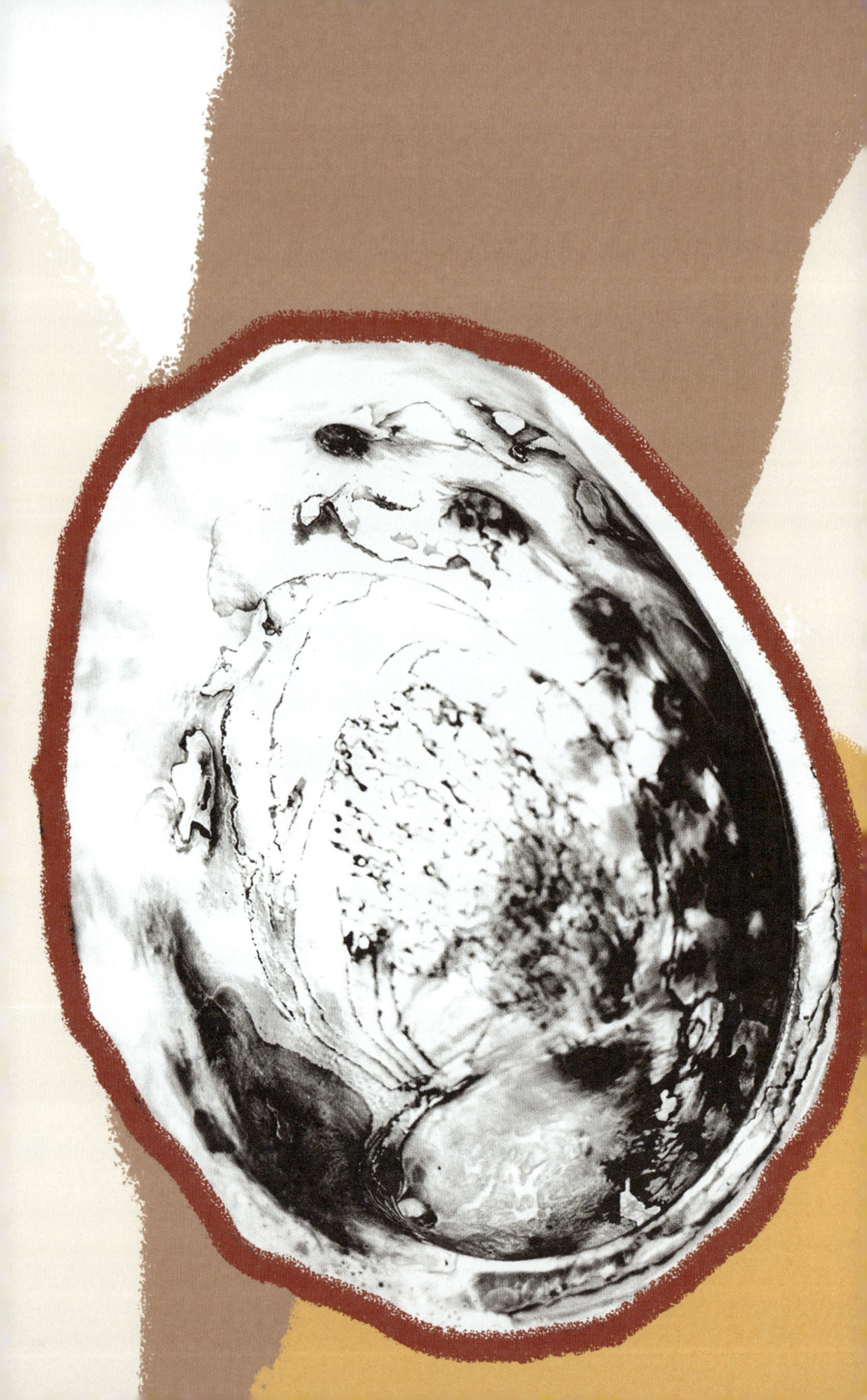

Afterword

By Rebecca Macarro

When I was asked to write the afterword as an editor, I soon realized the fog of the collective trauma we have experienced in the past four years prevents me from recalling exactly how the concept of publishing an anthology was conceived. I do believe it was originally my cousin, Camaray's idea of bringing together a group of women to write and reflect upon their experiences, so I was honored to be asked alongside our other cousin Avelaka, to edit the anthology and provide perspective on the evolving ways in which Indigenous Southern Californian women wished to be represented and seen. From there, the project officially began somewhere in 2018; I shared a shoddy little poster I made on Canva, casting out a wide net for artists to contribute to what was a perceived void in literature representing a variety of female Native Southern Californian voices. Since then, we have seen the publication of *Ka'm-t'em: A Journey Toward Healing*, also published by the Great Oak Press, which draws some parallels to *Yáamay* and further highlights the distinctions and diversity in our Southern Californian diaspora.

Being trusted with so many intimate stories and works of art was a privilege I will never forget: we pored over each submission with curiosity and care. Our wish has always been to not just hand you a curated construct of what an Indigenous woman from California looks like, but rather present the lived experiences to absorb in all of their beauty, allowing for the reader to interpret what separates us and weaves us together. We are not all mothers, we are not all heteronormative, we have not all grown up on the Rez, we do not fit one stereotype or another. What we do share, is the experience of being inextricably connected to a way of life, people and land that have existed for millennia. Some of us are bound to expectations that come with these ties, and some of us are reconnecting to them for the first time in our lives, and all of us have, or will make mistakes. By humanizing us, and amplifying these voices, we aspire to give hope to those who feel alone in this world, or marginalized, or like they don't belong.

Yáamay means to endure—It was a title we decided upon without much deliberation, as it felt like there was no other word to encompass what all of the pieces had in common. Here, endurance was no longer a term that meant merely survival, but rather a tool that each of us carry with us that allows us to adapt to our environments and strengthens our pride and identity. Yáamay represents the courage to stand in one's multiplicities and alchemize that wisdom to sustain ourselves and our future generations at a time when the future of our planet is uncertain and at times, enshrined in fear. We must remember that the world our ancestors lived in ended time and time again, and yet we are still here. We continue to build upon the paths they forged despite everyone betting against us. The words, songs, and visions we are still creating continue to feed our souls and as editors, we cultivated these stories like seeds.

The chapter titles of our anthology were chosen from several passages throughout the invaluable resource, *Yumáyk Yumáyk: Long Ago*, published in 1994 by Eric Elliott and Villiana Hyde, and inspired by previous works such as the chapters of the anthology *Remember the Earth*, edited by Gary Hobson, which separated its contributors into chapters according to the regions of North America that they hail from. Since our publication was intended to be centered on the tribes of Southern California, we chose 4 chapters that instead represented the idea of a life cycle. The concept of enduring as the namesake of this anthology and the central theme, examines the many struggles we encounter in life as Indigenous women and how we have chosen (or struggled) to overcome them: Most often, we have chosen creation over destruction time and time again. Each chapter represents the cycle of existence, death, rebirth, and growth, through the lens of our Indigenous language *Chamtéela*, but also through the words of an elder who is no longer with us, but had unique thoughts on the world that was rapidly changing around her. Villiana Hyde was a beloved teacher, knowledge and language keeper, auntie, and mother to my Godmother, Lorraine Hyde, who helped raise me from my infant years to age 18. The impact these women had on their communities is still felt today, and it felt empowering to be able to use Villiana's words to complement and give context to the many voices in this anthology. It is by no means a complete collection of all the wisdom, and languages that span the region of Southern California, but our wish is that each story can be reflected upon and interpreted through your own languages and teachings.

Most importantly, my hope as you read these stories, is that you understand what we have endured not just through generations, but as a small collective in the years it took to complete this project alone. We were very near the finish line in March 2020, as the world was consumed by pandemic, stalling nearly every aspect of life and setting in motion a new path for many of us. I have since relocated across the southern portion of the state to my homelands, Camaray has since completed several screenplays and filmed a short on her property nearby, and we all have suffered many losses. Most significantly, our beloved brother and cousin Mikah, passed away on February 18th, 2021. When a young, promising life is lost, it is so easy to feel defeated and powerless. The grief was so heart wrenching, it felt like holding on to this project meant I was grasping on to the experiences, lives, and stories I knew before everything changed for us. We will never be the same, yet we will always adapt, and this acceptance was one of the many lessons I learned from many of our contributors and forebears. Octavia Butler said in the *Parable of the Sower*, that "the only lasting truth is change."

Facing this grief, an enduring love we have for ones we have lost, those who are with us in this life and those yet to come, I am filled with gratitude releasing this anthology to the world. I love it for its imperfections, contradictions, beauty, and truth between these pages and I hope it resonates with you the way it did for us.

Bibliography

Anderson, Kat. *Tending the Wild: Native American Knowledge and the Management of California's Natural Resources*. University of California Press, 2013.

Carrico, Richard L. "Sociopolitical Aspects of the 1775 Revolt at Mission San Diego De Alcala." The Journal of San Diego History, vol. 43, no. 3, 1997, https://doi.org/https://sandiegohistory.org/journal/1997/july/missionrevolt/.

Castillo, Elias. *A Cross of Thorns: The Enslavement of California's Indians by the Spanish Missions*. Craven Street Books, 2017.

Dutschke, Dwight. "A History of American Indians of California: Introduction." *Five Views: An Ethnic Historic Site Survey for California*, State of California—the Resources Agency, Dept. of Parks and Recreation, Office of Historic Preservation, Sacramento, CA (P.O. Box 942896, Sacramento 94296-0001), 1988.

Getches, David H., et al. *Cases and Materials on Federal Indian Law*. West Academic Publishing, 2011.

Gutiérrez, Ramón, et al. *Contested Eden*. University of California Press, 1998.

Madley, Benjamin. "Op-Ed: It's Time to Acknowledge the Genocide of California's Indians." *Los Angeles Times*, 22 May 2016, https://www.latimes.com/opinion/op-ed/la-oe-madley-california-genocide-20160522-snap-story.html.

Hyde, Villiana Calac, and Eric Elliott. *Yumáyk Yumáyk*. University of California Press, 1994.

Pratt, Richard Henry. "The Advantages of Mingling Indians with Whites." *Carlisle Indian School Digital Resource Center*, Press of Geo. H. Ellis, https://carlisleindian.dickinson.edu/sites/all/files/docs-resources/CIS-Resources_1892-PrattSpeech.pdf.

United States Court of Appeals, Ninth Circuit. *Agua Caliente Band of Cahuilla Indians v. Coachella Valley Water District*. 7 Mar. 2017.

Villa, Sam. "History." *Gabrielino*, Gabrielino-Tongva Indian Tribe, https://gabrielinotribe.org/history/.

Contributor Bios

Annalisa Berrios is Payómkawichum from Pechanga. Her parents are Julie and Geno Salgado. Annalisa has always used writing as a way to heal. She believes it's important to have a healthy outlet and continue to grow. She continues to work for her people and to give back as many ways as possible. Annalisa strives to provide for her two sons and her community with strong, cultural teachings. Living without fear and embracing everything the Ancestors gave us is how Annalisa walks through life.

April Bouchard is a member of the Pechanga Band of Indians. She lives in Temecula, CA with her husband, three sons and their cat Hazel.

Emily Burgueno is an Iipai Siny/ Kumeyaay Woman from the Santa Ysabel Reservation. Brought up by her great grams, grandparents, parents, aunties, uncles, and siblings, Emily has learned from each of them to help her thrive in this modern world. She continues to walk her red road and tries to do better with each passing day by taking care of the land, processing seasonal foods/medicines, singing proudly, dancing strong, reversing assimilation by strengthening her traditional language, and expressing herself after many generations of being silenced.

Kelly Caballero is a singer-songwriter, performer, poet, and jeweler. Her body of work focuses primarily on highlighting the multifaceted and complex lives of Indigenous peoples born and raised in urban settings. She recently performed her poetry in collaboration with the great cellist, Yo-Yo Ma. Her work has been featured in partnership with The Ford Theater, Hollywood Climate Summit, The Hundreds Streetwear Brand, We Rise LA and much more. She continues to share her personal experience and stories of life, love and Indigenous resilience through her work as a Tongva woman.

Emily Clarke is a Cahuilla Native American writer, student, bead artist, activist, cordage instructor, and traditional Bird Dancer. Emily studies Creative Writing at UC Riverside and is currently writing work exploring modern Cahuilla identity, female anatomy, social justice, and human intimacy. "Shapeshifter" and "Thieved" can also be read in Volumes 32 (Issue 1) and 31 (Issue 2) of News From Native California.

Camaray Davalos (Payómkawichum/Xicana) graduated from Humboldt State University with a major in Native American Studies and a minor in Environmental Science Management. Currently, she's delved into the world of screenwriting, but considers herself a writer of many forms. Through her writing she aims to portray a uniquely genuine perspective of what it means to be Payómkawish living in today's world.

Megan Dorame is Tongva. She lives and writes in Orange County and Is active in the revitalization of the Tongva language. Follow her on Instagram: @meganmichelledorame and Twitter: @MeganDorame.

Marlene' Dusek is a Payómkawish, Kúupangawish, Kichámkawish, Xicana, and Czech woman who grew up on the Rincon Reservation. She graduated from Humboldt State University, which is located in Wiyot ancestral territory, with a Bachelor of Science in Environmental Science and Management with an emphasis in Environmental Planning and Policy, and a minor in Native American Studies. She is now back at HSU working towards her Masters in Environment and Community on a project called Payómkawichum Şúşngalum (Women), Chaamtúkmay (Our baskets), Our Relatives, Our Narratives. She holds many titles and interests, but is an Indigenous feminist scholar; Community organizer; Plant nerd and traditional gatherer & weaver; Photographer; Artist; Poet; Singer; & Environmental planner & GIS specialist.

Meadow Fuller is from the Pechanga Band of Indians. She is 20 years old, and currently enrolled in UCLA as an English major.

Dr. Theresa Gregor is an Assistant Professor in the Program in American Indian Studies at Cal State University Long Beach, aka Puvungna. She is Kumeyaay (Iipay Nation of Santa Ysabel) and Yoème from the Nejo shmulq. Her research analyzes the Kumeyaay language, experience, and stories from a cross-cultural perspective that takes into account the relationship between humans to nature and the world around them. Her creative and critical scholarship focuses on restor(y)ing the agency and power of Kumeyaay women in Kumeyaay origin stories. In particular her work examines perceptions of gender in Kumeyaay culture and highlights the roles and contributions of California Indian women. She currently resides in the foothills of the Angeles National Forest alongside the headwaters of the San Gabriel River in the homelands of the Tongva/Gabrieleno with her two children and her dog, Athena.

Casse Kihúut Alaniz is an Indigenous/Mexicana artist and filmmaker, who grew up in McAllen, Texas. She is Payómkawish from the Pechanga Band of Indians. Due to the separation from her native heritage growing up, racist representations of Indigenous peoples within the media became her own way of understanding that part of herself which she now aims to dismantle. Her work revolves around the understandings of identity and sexuality, as well as, representing unheard voices in film.

Míyexwe netéw'e Jenah Lattin! Jenah is descended from the Kuupangaxwichem and Acjachemen nations, and is a member of the Pala Band of Mission Indians. She is an aspiring nDn rights attorney, artist, and caregiver for her people.

Ericka Lopez is twenty one years old and from the Pechanga Band of Indians. She is a teacher's aid at Chammákilawish Pechanga School, a Northern Traditional Fancy Shawl dancer and a volunteer.

Avelakayawaywish Macarro is a sometimes editor and a consistent fan of this collection of poets and writers. She is driven by a desire to uplift and protect Native voices, and currently works at the University of Washington as the Director of Riverways Education Partnerships. She lives in Seattle, Washington and is now freelance-editing essays and short stories.

Rebecca Macarro (Payómkawichum/Pechanga Band of Indians) works in the Pechanga Tribal Youth Department and resides in her traditional homelands in Southern California. She is also a certified Doula and tempestuous Aquarius.

Poyomi McDarment is a Yokuts Artist who has been creating feminine content since the young age of three. She takes inspiration from women, plants and flowers, and is always trying to create an idea, situation, or something dream-like.

Alexis Munoa Dyer (Payómkawichum/Pechanga Band of Indians) is a musician, photographer, wife, mother, sister and auntie. She loves the power of healing found through artistic expression. Whether it's a song, visual imagery, or pine nut soup—she loves to feed the people.

Makayla Murillo is a descendent of the San Luis Rey Band of Mission Indians. She currently lives in Oceanside, California where her ancestors once occupied. She is interested in learning and preserving ancestral knowledge to educate future generations.

Amanda Nogales is a member of the Cahuilla Band of Indians, raised on the Pechanga Indian Reservation where she still resides. She has an A.S. in Child Development.

Genevra Munoa (Payómkawichum/Pechanga Band of Indians) recently completed her Masters of Education in Learning, Diversity and Urban Studies from Vanderbuilt University. She is a musician, singer, songwriter, weaver, beader, and roller skater.

Tristen Orosco is from the Pechanga Band of Indians. She is a mother, basket weaver, doula, and student midwife.

Kaitra Sbragia Inhabitant of the streams that lead to the ocean; descendant of Elsie Banks' side glances; raised by Sylvia Lira's raised eyebrows; formed from the red clay of Cactus Road.

Poyomi Thopishin (Jasmine Curlin) is from the Tule River Yokuts Band of California.

Nichole Vasquez-Sutter is an artist and an author, living with her husband and two young children in Northern California. Her family is Payómkawiichum of the Pechanga Band in Southern California.

Desiree Wetz is happily married with three children. She is Acjachemem, Luiseño, and Cahuilla blood. In her free time she crafts stories.

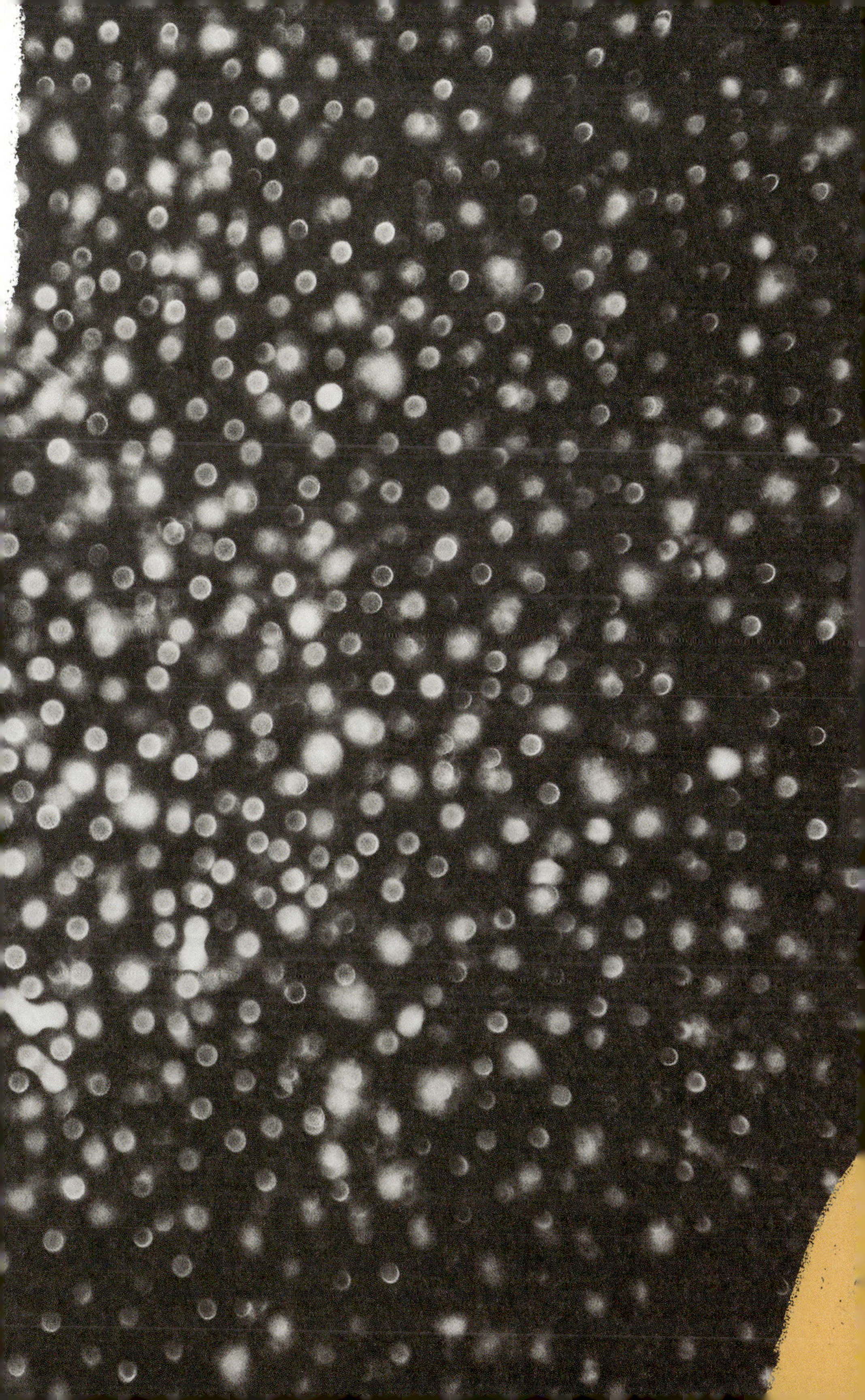

Lead Editors

Camaray Davalos, Avelaka Macarro,
and Rebecca Macarro on their coastal homelands.
For more information, follow @_yaamay_ on Instagram.